WORK IS HELL

A CARTOON BOOK BY MATT GROENING

OTHER BOOKS BY MATT GROENING

LOVE IS HELL
SCHOOL IS HELL
CHILDHOOD IS HELL
AKBAR & JEFF'S GUIDE TO LIFE
HOW TO GO TO HELL
THE ROAD TO HELL
THE BIG BOOK OF HELL
BINKY'S GUIDE TO LOVE
THE HUGE BOOK OF HELL

BOOKS BY MATT GROENING THAT APPEARED SOLELY IN THE AUTHOR'S DREAMS

PEOPLE ARE CRUNCHY
EVERYONE FOOLS THEIR OWN SELF

HARPERCOLLINSPUBLISHERS
77-85 FULHAM PALACE ROAD, HAMMERSMITH, LONDON W6 8JB
WWW.HARPERCOLLINS.CO.UK
THIS EDITION FIRST PUBLISHED 2004
1 3 5 7 9 8 6 4 2
ORIGINALLY PUBLISHED IN 1986 BY PANTHEON BOOKS,
A DIVISION OF RANDOM HOUSE, INC., NEW YORK.

ISBN 0 00 718130 2
PRINTED AND BOUND IN GREAT BRITAIN BY SCOTPRINT, HADDINGTON.

LIFE IN HELL

© 1985 BY MATT GROENING

LIFE IN HELL: AN INTRODUCTION

WHAT IS "LIFE IN HELL"?

AN AMUSING LITTLE TRIFLE OF A COMIC STRIP STARRING ASSORTED CRUDELY DRAWN RABBITS.

WHY SUCH A NEGATIVE TITLE?

I HAD JUST MOVED TO LOS ANGELES WHEN I THOUGHT IT UP.

WHAT ARE THE FIVE MAJOR THEMES OF "LIFE IN HELL"?

☆ LOVE
☆ SEX
☆ WORK
☆ DEATH
☆ LAUGHS

NOTES

DRAMATIS PERSONAE

BINKY — QUIT STARING AT MY EARS.
STAR OF "LIFE IN HELL." FLINCHES WHEN POKED. DISTINGUISHING FEATURES: BULGING EYES, OVERBITE, GROTESQUE EARS

SHEBA — QUIT STARING AT MY EARS.
BINKY'S EASILY IRKED GIRLFRIEND. PROPENSITY TO POKE BINKY. DISTINGUISHING FEATURES: BASICALLY BINKY IN FEMALE GARB.

BONGO — IT'S OK TO STARE AT MY EAR. I KNOW YOU CAN'T HELP IT.
BINKY'S ILLEGITIMATE SON. EVEN MORE ALIENATED THAN BINKY. DISTINGUISHING FEATURES: PRETTY OBVIOUS, ISN'T IT?

AKBAR & JEFF — I LOVE YOU / BUT I HATE YOU
BROTHERS OR LOVERS, OR POSSIBLY BOTH. NOTHING PERTURBS THEM. DISTINGUISHING FEATURES: FEZZES, BOTH EYES ON SAME SIDE OF HEAD.

HOW THE HELL DO YOU PRONOUNCE THE CARTOONIST'S NAME?

măt grā'nĭng

HINT: LAST NAME RHYMES WITH "COMPLAINING"

CAN THE CARTOONIST DRAW ANYTHING BESIDES RABBITS?

OH MY YES.

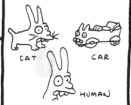

CAT   CAR

HUMAN

DOES THE CARTOONIST LOOK ANYTHING LIKE BINKY?

NOT REALLY.

SELF-PORTRAIT

LIFE IN HELL FUN FACTS

BINKIES IN HISTORY

IN WILLIAM MAKEPEACE THACKERAY'S NOVEL *VANITY FAIR* (1848), THERE'S A MINOR CHARACTER NAMED LORD BINKIE.

IN THE MOVIE THE LIGHT THAT FAILED (1939), RONALD COLMAN'S DOG IS NAMED BINKY.

IN THE LATTER HALF OF THE 20TH CENTURY, THERE WAS A POPULAR SWIMSUIT KNOWN AS THE BINKINI.

CAN THE CARTOONIST DRAW BINKY WITH HIS EYES CLOSED?

YOU DECIDE.

DID YOU KNOW?

MY NAME IS BINKY.

NOT BLINKY, PINKY, DINKY, BUNKY, ZIPPY, OR SNOOPY.

I HAVE ONE EAR SO YOU WON'T MISTAKE ME FOR BINKY.

IS THERE A "LIFE IN HELL" PHILOSOPHY?

OH MAIS OUI.

YOUR DAYS ARE NUMBERED.

IT'S LATER THAN YOU THINK.

WE'RE ALL DOOMED.

HAVE A NICE DAY.

LIFE IN HELL

QUICK-- WHILE THE BOSS ISN'T LOOKING-- CHECK OUT THIS CUTE AND CUDDLY 10-PART CARTOON MINISERIES.

WORK IS HELL

CHAPTER 1:
UP AND AT 'EM!

PSST!

WARNING

CHUCKLING TOO INTENSELY AT THIS COMIC STRIP COULD RESULT IN EARLY TERMINATION

QUESTIONS

WHAT DO I WANT TO BE IF I GROW UP? WHY WOULD ANYONE WANT TO HIRE ME? WHAT IF I MAKE THE WRONG CAREER CHOICE? WHAT IF I DON'T LIKE MY JOB? HOW COME I HAVE SUCH BAD LUCK? HOW CAN I GET RICH? DOES LIFE HAVE TO BE THIS TEDIOUS? WHEN IS MY COFFEE BREAK? WHY ME?

ANSWER: GET BACK TO WORK.

THE FACE OF WORK

STRANGE SENSATION THAT TIME HAS SLOWED TO A CRAWL AND YET YOUR WHOLE LIFE IS PASSING BEFORE YOUR EYES

SUPPRESSED RAGE

THROBBING HEADACHE

VACANT LOOK

BAGS UNDER EYES

THE SNIFFLES

SCALDED TONGUE

BAD BREATH

PERMANENT SLOUCH

LOWER BACK PAIN

RECTAL ITCH

READ 'EM. MEMORIZE 'EM. FILE 'EM.

WORK PROVERBS

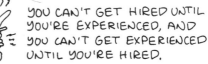

IT'S A DOG-EAT-DOG WORLD OUT THERE.

TIME IS MONEY.

YOU CAN'T GET HIRED UNTIL YOU'RE EXPERIENCED, AND YOU CAN'T GET EXPERIENCED UNTIL YOU'RE HIRED.

A RAISE? YOU'RE LUCKY WE DON'T FIRE YOU.

GET BACK TO WORK.

BASIC WORK TOOLS

YOU WILL NEED:

A SCARY ALARM CLOCK

WORK IS HELL

HOT SLUDGY COFFEE

CARCINOGENIC SWEETENER (FOR COFFEE)

A BIG SMILE

THE BENEFITS OF WORK

VACATION

PAYCHECK

YESSIR

RIGHT AWAY SIR

HUMILITY

A JOB WELL DONE

EARLY GRAVE

ETERNAL PEACE

YOU ARE NOT ALONE

THERE'S SOMEONE IN THE NEXT CUBICLE WHO THINKS JUST LIKE YOU.

I DON'T KNOW HOW LONG I CAN LAST IN THIS PLACE.

I DON'T KNOW HOW LONG YOU CAN LAST IN THIS PLACE EITHER.

WORKER'S DIARY

	MON	TUE	WED
	Got up. Went to work. Came home. Watched TV. Went to bed.	Got up. Went to work. Came home. Watched TV. Went to bed.	Got up. Went to work. Came home. Watched TV. Went to bed.

THU	FRI	SAT	SUN
Got up. Went to work. Came home. Watched TV. Went to bed.	Got up. Went to work. Cashed paycheck. Came home. Got drunk.	Don't remember.	Don't remember.

JUST REMEMBER:
IF YOU DON'T LIKE IT

YOU CAN LUMP IT.

NEXT: MORE OF THE SAME.

LIFE IN HELL

MOVE IT

YEAH, MOVE IT

WORK IS HELL

1 GROSS · WORK IS HELL · WORK IS HELL · WORK IS HELL

CHAPTER 2:
HOW TO FACE UP TO YOUR FIRST JOB

DON'T BE A FOOL, STAY IN SCHOOL

HOW MANY TIMES HAVE YOU HEARD THAT WISE OLD RHYME? PLENTY, WE BET. AND THERE'S A REASON.

SCHOOL IS GOOD. SCHOOL IS IMPORTANT. SCHOOLS PREPARES YOU FOR THE FUTURE. BY SITTING QUIETLY IN NEAT ROWS FOR LONG PERIODS OF TIME DOING EXACTLY WHAT YOU ARE TOLD IN SCHOOL, YOU ARE PREPARING TO SIT QUIETLY IN NEAT ROWS FOR LONG PERIODS OF TIME DOING EXACTLY WHAT YOU ARE TOLD AS AN ADULT.

AND REMEMBER:

IF YOU STAY IN SCHOOL FOR YEARS AND YEARS, YOU'LL DELAY (FOR AWHILE) YOUR WORST WORKING FEARS

PREPARE FOR DISAPPOINTMENT

INVENTORIED THE WHOLE WAREHOUSE, BOSS.

HMMM.... WE'RE SHORT A COUPLE XP-13s. BETTER COUNT EVERYTHING AGAIN.

HELL CO

THAT'S RIGHT. WORK IS NOT ALL GRAVY AND BONUS POINTS. AT MOMENTS IT CAN BE FRUSTRATING, DEGRADING, AND DOWNRIGHT IRKSOME. DO YOU KNOW WHAT TOP BUSINESS LEADERS HAVE TO SAY ABOUT THIS? "TOUGH BEANS, PAL." THINK ABOUT IT.

IF YOU CAN KEEP YOUR EXPECTATIONS TINY YOU'LL GO THROUGH LIFE WITHOUT BEING SO WHINY.

WHAT KIND OF WORK DO YOU REALLY WANT TO DO FOR THE REST OF YOUR LIFE?

DON'T TAKE THIS QUESTION LIGHTLY. THE ANSWER COULD VERY WELL AFFECT YOUR ENTIRE FUTURE.

DO YOU TAKE PLEASURE IN ADDING UP COLUMN AFTER COLUMN OF MEANINGLESS NUMBERS, OR IS YOUR IDEA OF A GOOD TIME WADING THROUGH MOUNTAINS OF BUREAUCRATIC GIBBERISH?

HMMM.... 273965... WOW....

WHAT A FASCINATING MEMO

OH MY BACK

OH MY BACK

MY STOMACH

MY ASS

DO YOU ENJOY UTTERLY MINDLESS HEAVY MANUAL LABOR, OR WOULD YOU RATHER SIT ON YOUR BUTT BEHIND A DESK FOR DECADES WHILE YOUR ATERIES HARDEN AND YOUR MUSCLES TURN TO MUSH?

DO YOU WANT TO WORK IN AN OFFICE FULL OF DEVIOUS, BITTER, NERVOUS WRECKS WHO ALL RESENT EACH OTHER, OR WOULD YOU RATHER TOIL ALONE IN A WINDOWLESS ROOM WITH NO DISTRACTIONS AND BE WATCHED BY A SECURITY CAMERA?

YOU SEE LETTERMAN LAST NIGHT? WOTTA RIOT

I NEVER STAY UP THAT LATE

YOU SEE LETTERMAN LAST NIGHT? LOTSA LAUGHS

ALL RIGHT, FUNTIME'S OVER

BACK TO WORK

GET THE LEAD OUT

GO, GO, GO!

WIPE THAT STUPID LOOK OFF YOUR FACE

NOW

DO YOU ENJOY BEING BULLIED BY SEVERAL SMALL BOSSES, OR WOULD YOU RATHER BE BULLIED BY ONE BIG BOSS?

ARE YOU WILLING TO GIVE UP ALL YOUR YOUTHFUL WILD DREAMS AND SOARING AMBITIONS FOR A BORING BUT SECURE JOB, OR WOULD YOU RATHER REFRAIN FROM SELLING OUT AND SPEND THE REST OF YOUR LIFE WORKING AT A SERIES OF WORTHLESS, MARGINAL JOBS WITH NO FUTURE ON THE SLIM CHANCE THAT SOMEDAY YOUR LUCK WILL MIRACULOUSLY CHANGE?

AT LEAST I'M HAPPY, SORT OF

AT LEAST I'M NOT JUST SORT OF HAPPY, SORT OF

THE SECRET OF SUCCESS

1. GET A JOB.
2. GET A BETTER JOB.
3. GET AN EVEN BETTER JOB.

REPEAT IF NECESSARY

NEXT: THE NINE TYPES OF BOSSES

LIFE IN HELL

© 1985 BY MATT GROENING

WORK IS HELL

NO IT ISN'T. GET BACK TO WORK.

CHAPTER 3: THE 9 TYPES OF BOSSES

HEY LOUIE!! GET A LOADA THIS SILLY CARTOON ABOUT TRIVIAL ON-THE-JOB ANXIETIES

"THE ANGRY BEHEMOTH"

I DON'T PAY YOU TO THINK. I PAY YOU TO CRINGE WHILE I SCREAM AND RANT.

ALSO KNOWN AS: THE APE, MR. TANTRUM, GRUMPY, THE GROUCH, OL' FLARING NOSTRILS.
HOW TO HANDLE: HIDE, MAKE SNICKERING REMARKS TO CO-WORKERS.
WARNING: STUPIDER THAN S/HE LOOKS.

"THE ROBOT FROM PLANET X"

YOUR 10-MINUTE BREAK IS OVER IN 5 MINUTES.

ALSO KNOWN AS: THE BUREAUCRAT, THE WATCHER, THE THING WITH THE X-RAY EYES, THE LIVING DEAD, ICE MACHINE, ZOMBIE (OR ZOMBINA)
HOW TO HANDLE: CONCEAL ALL FEELINGS.
WARNING: CONTAGIOUS.

"MR. SOFTY"

GOSH, I DON'T KNOW ABOUT THAT. I'LL JUST HAVE TO THINK ABOUT IT FOR AWHILE. I JUST ₩₩ ₥ ～ ～₩ ～ ₥ ～

ALSO KNOWN AS: WHATSITSNAME, SQUISHY, THE PUSHOVER, JELLYFISH, MOVING TARGET.
HOW TO HANDLE: GENTLY.
WARNING: CAUSES DROWSINESS.

"THE SLIPPERY EEL"

JUST KEEP QUIET AND DO YOUR JOB AND 12 TO 24 MONTHS FROM NOW I THINK YOU'RE DUE FOR A SURPRISE.

NO PROMISES.

ALSO KNOWN AS: THE MANIPULATOR, THE LIAR, THE SNEAK, THE GENIUS.
HOW TO HANDLE: RUN FOR YOUR LIFE.
WARNING: S/HE'S EVERYWHERE.

"THE GREAT UNKNOWN"

DO NOT DISTURB

ALSO KNOWN AS: THE LURKING UNKNOWN, THE CREEPING UNKNOWN, THE HIDING UNKNOWN.
HOW TO HANDLE: WATCH AND WAIT.
WARNING: BITES WHEN CORNERED.

"THE SPITTING COBRA"

GOOD MORNING.

WHAT AN UGLY SHIRT.

IT FIGURES.

OH, CHEER UP.

ALSO KNOWN AS: THE SNAPPING TURTLE, POISON IVY, THE PESKY IRRITANT, OH NO.
HOW TO HANDLE: BOIL WITH RAGE (SILENTLY).
WARNING: YOUR HEAD MAY EXPLODE.

"THE HORNY TOAD"

LET'S FORGET ABOUT WORK AND JUST RELAX.

HOW ABOUT A LITTLE DRINK?

THIS COULD BE YOUR BIG BREAK.

JUST KIDDING. JEEZ, RELAX.

ALSO KNOWN AS: SLEAZEBUCKET, SLIMEBALL, SCUMBAG, HANDSOME DEVIL.
HOW TO HANDLE: SAY FERGIT IT.
WARNING: COULD RESULT IN TERMINATION, OR WORSE-- MARRIAGE.

"WONDER BOSS"

GOOD NEWS, EVERYONE. BECAUSE OF A GREAT YEAR OF FUN AND PROFITS, I HAVE HEFTY BONUSES AND A GENEROUS PROFIT-SHARING PLAN FOR ALL OF YOU!

ALSO KNOWN AS: I DON'T BELIEVE IT, GOD, PERFECTION, WHAT A GUY (OR GAL)
HOW TO HANDLE: THROW CAUTION TO THE WIND.
WARNING: COULD BE THE SLIPPERY EEL IN DISGUISE.

"THE PSYCHOTIC BOSS-MONSTER FROM HELL"

HOW DARE YOU DUCK WHEN I THROW THINGS AT YOU!!

ALSO KNOWN AS: THE RAMPAGING BEAST-THING, UNREASONABLE, HERE COMES TROUBLE, YESSIR RIGHT AWAY SIR.
HOW TO HANDLE: COWER, HOPE FOR HEART ATTACK.
WARNING: DON'T LET IT SEE THIS CARTOON.

LIFE IN HELL

© 1985 BY MATT GROENING

"WORK IS HELL." — "MGMPH" — "BE RIGHT BACK."

CHAPTER 4: THE 81 TYPES OF EMPLOYEES

"BINKY'S FOMENTING WORKER DISSATISFACTION AGAIN, SIR." — "SEND THAT LITTLE SNEAK IN HERE."

THE TUNELESS WHISTLER	THE SUGARLESS-GUM SNAPPER	GIGGLES	THE FLASHY HOTSHOT	THE SMILING IDEA-STEALER	THE SMILING BACKSTABBER	THE BOOTLICKING TOADY	THE RACIST JOKESTER	THE BOSS'S NEPHEW
THE HUNGOVER MESSENGER	THE STONE-FACED VICE PRESIDENT	THE HUFFY OFFICE MANAGER	THE BEADY-EYED GRUDGE-HOLDER	THE RESENTFUL OAF	THE QUEEN BEE	THE HAPPY-GO-LUCKY CLERK	THE SCATTER BRAIN	THE MARRIED RECEPTIONIST
THE DIETING SECRETARY	THE UNHAPPY COMPUTER REPAIR PERSON	THE TYRANNICAL PIPSQUEAK	THE POMPOUS WADDLER	THE WIDE-EYED INTERN	THE NAMELESS FILE CLERK	THE DERISIVE CRITIC	THE SULLEN TEMPORARY SECRETARY	THE OFFICE OUTCAST
THE BOSS'S FROSTY SECRETARY	THE VERY UNHAPPY COPY-MACHINE REPAIRPERSON	THE SECRET DRUNK	THE NOT-SO-SECRET DRUNK	THE ANGRY MUMBLING JANITOR	THE YELLING DEPARTMENT CHIEF	THE INCOMPETENT MANAGER	THE WRETCHED DRONE	THE INSUFFERABLE OFFICE WISEGUY
THE BREEZY SALES REP	THE INSANE SALES REP	THE SUICIDAL SALES REP	THE ABUSIVE SALES MANAGER	THE MERE COG IN THE MACHINE	THE SQUEAKY WHEEL	THE SNEAKY THIEF	THE FLUNKY	THE SLAVE
THE ANONYMOUS DRONE	THE YOUNG HOPEFUL	THE YOUNG HOPELESS	THE YOUNG HATEFUL	THE BOSS'S SPY	THE NERVOUS BOOKKEEPER	THE BARKING LOADING-DOCK FOREMAN	THE GRUNTING LOADING-DOCK WORKER	THE STONED LOADING-DOCK WORKER
THE SHAKING NEWCOMER	THE BITTER OLDTIMER	THE OFFICE SNOOP	THE CLOCK WATCHER	THE COFFEE-SIPPER	THE DAYDREAMER	THE DAWDLER	THE TIGHT-LIPPED RELIGIOUS FANATIC	DOG BREATH
THE FASHION PLATE	THE SLOB	THE WOMAN WHO DRESSES SCANDALOUSLY	THE HORRIBLE TOUPÉ WEARER	THE CARPING MANAGER	THE SWAGGERING ASSISTANT MANAGER	THE BABBLING FOOL	THE PASSIVE-AGGRESSIVE PEON	THE SCHEMER
THE SILENT GRUMP	THE NICE GUY	THE SWEET GAL	THE VAGUELY DISSATISFIED	THE DAZED FOLLOWER	THE SEETHING TEETH-GRITTER	THE HEADACHE COLLECTOR	THE LIFE-WASTING SLUGGARD	PASTE YOUR PHOTO HERE

© 1985 BY MATT GROENING

WORK IS HELL

RAISE? YOU'RE LUCKY WE DON'T FIRE YOU. GET BACK TO WORK.

CHAPTER 5:
HOW TO GET ALONG WITH ALL THE JERKS AT YOUR CRUMMY JOB

WHY CAN'T YOU JUST TRY TO BE A TEAM PLAYER?

KEEP YOUR BOSS HAPPY

BOSSES HAVE NEEDS, TOO. THEY NEED TO INSULT YOU, DEGRADE YOU, TREAT YOU LIKE A CHILD, AND HUMILIATE YOU IN FRONT OF YOUR CO-WORKERS. DON'T TAKE IT PERSONALLY. JUST LEARN TO CONCEAL YOUR THOUGHTS, FEELINGS, OPINIONS, HOPES, AND AMBITIONS, AND YOU'LL PROBABLY DO OKAY.
WHEN THE BOSS YELLS, JUST THINK ABOUT THE FUTURE.

YOU DID IT WRONG AGAIN, STUPID

BE THE PERFECT EMPLOYEE

PRACTICE THESE SENTENCES UNTIL YOU CAN SAY THEM WITHOUT THINKING.

I DON'T WORRY MUCH ABOUT ANYTHING.

I FAVOR POLITICS THAT REWARD THE RICH AND PUNISH THE POOR.

I DON'T CARE ABOUT ART OR MUSIC OR BOOKS.

I'M HAPPY WITH THINGS JUST THE WAY THEY ARE.

I THINK THE BOSS'S JOKES ARE FUNNY.

HOW TO SHOW A CO-WORKER YOUR DISPLEASURE WITHOUT ACTUALLY SAYING ANYTHING

1. STIFFEN YOUR BODY WHEN APPROACHED.
2. PURSE YOUR LIPS.
3. BECOME SUDDENLY ENTRANCED IN YOUR OWN WORK.
4. DRAW AIR ABRUPTLY INTO YOUR NOSE, CREATING A SUBTLE BUT DISTINCTIVE SNIFFING EFFECT.
5. WALK OUT OF THE ROOM AS IF YOU'VE GOT A BROOM UP YOUR ASS.

HI!

OH. HI.

YOU CAN AFFECT THE MOODS OF OTHERS

I JUST GOT A RAISE!!

OH, REALLY? THAT'S GREAT.

I JUST GOT DEMOTED!

OH, REALLY? THAT'S TOO BAD.

SHARE THE GOOD TIMES

CARE FOR ONE OF MY CHEWABLE ANTACID TABLETS?

THEY'RE MINTY.

SHARE THE BAD TIMES

I -- I JUST GOT FIRED.

GEE, THAT'S ROUGH.

LET'S MEET AT RANDOM ON THE STREET SEVERAL YEARS FROM NOW AND NOT REMEMBER EACH OTHER'S NAME.

HOW TO DECODE YOUR CO-WORKERS' INSIPID CHATTER

WHEN THEY SAY:	THEY REALLY MEAN:
YOU LOOK CHEERFUL THIS MORNING.	WHAT THE HELL IS WRONG WITH YOU?
GEE, THE BOSS SURE CHEWED YOU OUT.	HA HA HA HA HA HA
G'NIGHT, EVERYBODY! HAVE A GOOD ONE! SEE YOU TOMORROW!	GO FUCK YOURSELVES.

IN CONCLUSION:

	YOUR BOSS IS INSANE.
	YOUR CO-WORKERS ARE INSANE.
	YOU'RE FINALLY BEGINNING TO FIT IN.

LIFE IN HELL

WELL, I SAY WORK IS HELLO, BOSS!

CHAPTER 6:
JUST HOW BAD IS YOUR JOB?

GOOD NEWS, BOYS. ONLY ONE OF YOU HAS TO WORK LATE TONIGHT.

YAY!!!

BAD JOB CHECKLIST

PLACE AN "X" IN EACH APPROPRIATE BOX. USE YOUR OWN PENCIL. PLEASE DO NOT CRUMPLE THIS CHECKLIST. IT IS ONLY A CARTOON.

ULP

1. HEALTH
- ☐ WORK WITH DANGEROUS, NOXIOUS CHEMICALS
- ☐ WORK WITH DANGEROUS, NOXIOUS CO-WORKERS

2. WORK OVERLOAD
- ☐ LAUGHABLY UNREALISTIC DEADLINES
- ☐ WORK IS PILED ON UNTIL YOUR HEAD EXPLODES

3. WORK UNDERLOAD
- ☐ REQUIRED TO LOOK BUSY WHEN THERE'S NOTHING TO DO
- ☐ BRAIN IS ATROPHYING FROM IDLENESS

4. TIME PRESSURES
- ☐ HAVE TO WORK TOO FAST
- ☐ HAVE TO WORK TOO SLOW
- ☐ HAVE TO WORK LIKE A MACHINE
- ☐ DON'T HAVE TIME TO FINISH THIS CHECKLIST

QUIT GOOFIN OFF

---

5. SECURITY
- ☐ THREAT OF BEING FIRED OR LAID OFF DANGLED OVER YOUR HEAD
- ☐ RIDICULOUS HEALTH PLAN
- ☐ PREPOSTEROUS PENSION PLAN
- ☐ PETITE FINANCIAL REWARDS

LIKE IT OR... LIKE IT OR... LUMP IT?

DON'T INTERRUPT.

6. CO-WORKERS
- ☐ UNFRIENDLY CO-WORKERS
- ☐ MALICIOUS CO-WORKERS
- ☐ CO-WORKERS EVEN MORE SCREWED UP THAN YOU

SORRY WE FORGOT YER BIRTHDAY LAST WEEK.

MAYBE NEXT YEAR.

7. BOREDOM
- ☐ JOB REQUIRES THE BRAINS OF A SLOW CHIMP
- ☐ WORK SEEMS POINTLESS
- ☐ JOB REQUIRES TEDIOUS TASKS BE DONE OVER AND OVER UNTIL YOU WANT TO SCREAM.

---

8. THE BOSS
- ☐ SAYS NOTHING
- ☐ STARES
- ☐ HAS VEINS IN FOREHEAD THAT THROB MENACINGLY
- ☐ TELLS HORRIBLE JOKES
- ☐ TAKES PLEASURE IN DESTROYING WHAT LITTLE ENJOYMENT YOU GET OUT OF LIFE
- ☐ BREATH THAT COULD KILL 1,000 ELVES

DJA HEAR THE ONE ABOUT THE STUPID WOMAN DRIVER?

HA HA TELL IT AGAIN BOSS

9. HOPELESSNESS
- ☐ NO HOPE FOR PROMOTION
- ☐ NO HOPE FOR RAISE
- ☐ NO HOPE FOR LEARNING
- ☐ NO HOPE FOR HAPPINESS
- ☐ NO HOPE FOR ESCAPE

HEY-- QUITTING TIME WAS 3 HOURS AGO!! GO HOME!!!

THE WORK'LL BE WAITING FOR YOU....

10. MENTAL PROBLEMS

HA HA

HA

- ☐ CHRONIC FATIGUE
- ☐ EMBITTERED CYNICISM
- ☐ SNEERING HATEFULNESS
- ☐ SO APATHETIC THIS CARTOON BARELY REGISTERS IN YOUR BENUMBED LITTLE BRAIN
- ☐ SO CLOSE TO COMPLETELY FLIPPING OUT THAT THIS CARTOON MAKES YOU LAUGH MIRTHLESSLY AND SQUIRM LIKE AN ITCHY BEAR CUB

---

11. PHYSICAL PROBLEMS
- ☐ SLUMPED SHOULDERS
- ☐ BACK ACHE
- ☐ MOUTH DRY AS A GULCH
- ☐ PUKING
- ☐ DEATH

DEAD. LUCKY STIFF.

I GET HIS STAPLER.

12. MISCELLANEOUS

WHISTLE WHILE YOU WORK ♫

NO WHISTLING.

- ☐ WHY ME?
- ☐ IF ONLY... IF ONLY...
- ☐ GOD HATES ME
- ☐ WHY BOTHER?
- ☐ WHO CARES?
- ☐ SO WHAT?
- ☐ LIFE IS BUT A DREAM

13. PHILOSOPHY OF LIFE

TWO STATEMENTS FOLLOW. CHECK THE ONE THAT MOST CLOSELY DESCRIBES YOUR CURRENT OUTLOOK.

- ☐ MISERY LOVES COMPANY.
- ☐ THE COMPANY LOVES MISERY.

INTERPRETING YOUR SCORE

- • NO BOXES CHECKED: YOU MAY HAVE A GOOD JOB, BUT REST ASSURED THAT EVERYONE ELSE HATES YOU.
- • SOME BOXES CHECKED: PERHAPS YOU SHOULD TRY TO GET A BETTER JOB.
- • ALL BOXES CHECKED: OH, CHEER UP.

(PSSST-- WORK IS HELL)

CHAPTER 8:
SO YOU GOT YOURSELF FIRED

NO IT ISN'T.

YOU'RE FIRED.

THE PAINFUL HUMILIATION OF IT ALL

GETTING SACKED. RECEIVING THE BOOT. GETTING KICKED OUT. GOING ON A PERMANENT VACATION. GETTING THE AXE. RECEIVING ONE'S WALKING PAPERS. GETTING THE PINK SLIP. HAVING THE ROLLERS PUT UNDER YOU. GETTING DEJOBBED.

THEY ALL MEAN JUST ONE THING.

YOU ARE DEAD MEAT ON A STICK.

YOU'RE FIRED!

WHO, ME?

FIG. ONE. TYPICAL.

THINGS TO SAY IF YOU JUST GOT FIRED

I -- JUST -- GOT -- FIRED.

PLEASE! JUST ONE MORE CHANCE!!!

SO LONG, SUCKERS.

I JUST QUIT MY JOB, EVERYONE! TOODLES!!

HAVE YOU EVER SEEN SOMEONE GET FIRED?

IT'S NOT A PRETTY SIGHT. THE VICTIM STAGGERS JERKILY FORWARD WITH A STRANGE GLASSY LOOK, AS IF IN ACUTE SHOCK, EXTREME SHAME, UTTER CONFUSION, OR A COMBO PLATTER OF ALL THREE.

YOU SAY:

WHAT'S WITH YOU, PAL?

HE OR SHE GURGLES:

I -- JUST -- GOT -- CANNED.

AND THEN YOU BOTH GET VERY QUIET.

REMEMBER:

THE PERSON WHO HAS BEEN FIRED IS PROBABLY UPSET. DO NOT EXPECT NORMAL BEHAVIOR -- JUST TRY TO STAY CLEAR. IF THE PERSON WHO HAS BEEN FIRED IS YOU, YOU MUST REALIZE YOU ARE OUT OF YOUR GODDAMNED MIND. DO NOT DO ANYTHING RASH. DO NOT:

☐ KILL YOURSELF. ☐ KILL YOUR BOSS.
☐ KILL EVERYONE YOU WORK WITH, EVEN THE RECEPTIONIST WHO WAS ALWAYS NICE TO YOU.
☐ KILL YOUR FAMILY. ☐ KILL YOUR PETS.

THINGS TO SAY TO A PERSON WHO'S JUST BEEN FIRED

NICE KNOWIN' YA.

NOW WHAT'RE YOU GONNA DO?

SURE GLAD I AIN'T YOU.

WELL -- GOTTA GO.

SEE YOU AROUND SOMETIME.

NOW WHAT?

YOU'RE OUT ON YOUR ASS AND FEELING LOUSY. BUT DON'T LOSE YOUR SELF-RESPECT, WHATEVER YOU DO. CRAWL AWAY WITH DIGNITY AND WEEP AND MOAN IN THE PRIVACY OF THE HOME YOU CAN SUDDENLY NO LONGER AFFORD. THINGS ARE NOT TOTALLY HOPELESS. THEY JUST SEEM THAT WAY. AND THEY WILL PROBABLY CONTINUE TO SEEM THAT WAY FOR A LONG, LONG TIME.

BUCK UP!

IT'S TIME TO GET ANOTHER JOB. THIS TIME, CHANGE YOUR ATTITUDE. GROVEL A BIT MORE. DEVELOP A POSITIVE, GO-WITH-THE-FLOW PHILOSOPHY. AT EACH JOB INTERVIEW, TRY TO BE RELAXED. DON'T APPEAR OVERANXIOUS. ADOPT A CAREFREE OUTLOOK. SAY:

HERE WE GO AGAIN.

AND MAYBE -- JUST MAYBE -- YOU'LL LIVE HAPPILY EVER AFTER.

LIFE IN HELL

ADDRESS ALL CORRESPONDENCE TO:
P.O. BOX 36E64
LOS ANGELES, CA 90036
USA

©1985 BY MATT GROENING

WORK IS HELL

GRRR

CHAPTER 9:

HOW TO TELL EVERYONE OFF, GO INTO BUSINESS FOR YOURSELF, BE COMPLETELY FULFILLED, AND STARVE TO DEATH

GRREEAT TIE YOU HAVE ON THIS MORNIN', BOSS.

THERE YOU SIT

AT YOUR DESK, SEETHING AND STEWING, WHILE A VAGUE, UNNAMEABLE SENSATION EATS AWAY AT YOU. IT'S NOT QUITE NAUSEA, IT'S NOT QUITE SUFFOCATION --JUST A SORT OF SICKLY FEELING IN THE GUT, LIKE MAYBE LIFE IS PASSING YOU BY, AND YOU ARE TRAPPED--

TRAPPED BY CRUEL FATE, BY THE GREED OF OTHERS, BY AN UNFAIR ECONOMIC SYSTEM, AND BY YOUR OWN CUDDLY NICENESS. BUT DEEP DOWN YOU HAVE A WHOLE SLEW OF SHAMEFUL YEARNINGS--DON'T DENY IT--AND ONE OF THOSE SECRET DESIRES IS TO TELL EVERYONE TO GO STRAIGHT TO HELL AND GO INTO BUSINESS FOR YOURSELF. "I'M FED UP WITH THIS HORRIBLE SITUATION I FIND MYSELF IN," YOU WHISPER TO YOURSELF, MAKING SURE NO ONE CAN SEE YOUR LIPS MOVING. "I WANT TO BE MY OWN BOSS FOR ONCE!" YOU SCREAM IN THE SILENCE OF YOUR OWN

FEVERISH BRAIN, MAKING SURE NO ONE CAN SEE YOUR HEAD THROB. YOU FEEL HARASSED FROM ABOVE BY CONTEMPTUOUS SUPERIORS, AND PECKED AT FROM BELOW BY CONNIVING SUBORDINATES WHO WOULD LIKE NOTHING BETTER THAN TO SEE YOU FAIL. BUT THAT AIN'T A-GOIN' TO HAPPEN! YOU'LL SHOW 'EM!!

YOU'LL SHOW ALL OF 'EM!!! ALL YOUR SO-CALLED FRIENDS, EVEN THAT HIGH-SCHOOL GUIDANCE COUNSELOR WHO TOLD YOU TO THINK SMALL-- AND ESPECIALLY YOUR PARENTS!!

BUT WAIT!!! WHAT IF--WHAT IF YOU DO FAIL?? THEN THEY'D BE RIGHT-- THEY TOLD YOU IT WOULD NEVER WORK, THEY TOLD YOU TO DO WHAT YOU WERE TOLD, THEY WHO LAUGHED BEHIND YOUR BACK ARE NOW LAUGHING IN FRONT OF YOUR FACE!!!

(WHAT A HORRIBLE THOUGHT.) BETTER JUST TRY TO FIT IN AND DO YOUR JOB! IT'S NOT SO BAD HERE! YOU'VE GOT A MIGHTY GENEROUS PENSION PLAN,

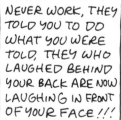

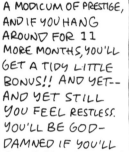

A MODICUM OF PRESTIGE, AND IF YOU HANG AROUND FOR 11 MORE MONTHS, YOU'LL GET A TIDY LITTLE BONUS!! AND YET-- AND YET STILL YOU FEEL RESTLESS. YOU'LL BE GOD-DAMNED IF YOU'LL SIT THROUGH ANOTHER POINTLESS COMMITTEE MEETING, LISTENING TO THOSE IDIOTS BABBLE ON AND ON

AND ON AND ON. YOU'RE NO WORM! YOU WERE MEANT FOR ADVENTURE AND INDEPENDENCE! HOW THE HELL DID YOU END UP IN THIS PREDICAMENT, ANYWAY? WHAT COULD YOU HAVE POSSIBLY DONE TO DESERVE THIS?

IT'S TIME TO PACK IT ALL IN AND GET THE HELL OUT OF HERE!! IT'S TIME TO TAKE CHARGE OF YOUR LIFE!! IT'S TIME TO BE A FULL-FLEDGED AUTONOMOUS HUMAN BEING!!! IT'S TIME TO GET

BACK TO WORK--COFFEE BREAK'S OVER.

NEXT: WORK IS HELL-- THE DEPRESSING CONCLUSION

LIFE IN HELL

I SAID, WORK IS HELL, YOU OLD GOAT!!

CHAPTER 10 (FINAL CHAPTER):
THE GAME OF WORK

I DIDN'T MEAN IT I DIDN'T MEAN IT

YOUR BED

BEGIN AND END HERE

LATE AGAIN
GULP DOWN A CUP OF SCALDING INSTANT COFFEE, RUN OUT THE DOOR IN A DISHEVELED STATE, FIGHT THE MORNING TRAFFIC JAM, AND ARRIVE AT WORK COMPLETELY FRAZZLED WITH ONLY EIGHT HOURS TO GO.

GET SCREAMED AT THE MOMENT YOU WALK IN.
TOP O' THE MORNIN' TO YOU, BOSS
OH SHUT UP

GET YOUR WORK EVALUATED.
YOU SCREWED UP EVERYTHING AGAIN, STUPID!!

DISCOVER THE TREACHERY OF A CO-WORKER WHO HAS SQUEALED ON YOU TO THE BOSS.
HE DID IT HE DID IT

COFFEE BREAK!
NON-DAIRY CREME?   WORK'D BE HELL   ARTIFICIAL SWEETENER?

FIGHT TRAFFIC ALL THE WAY HOME. EAT A LOUSY DINNER, FIGHT WITH YOUR SPOUSE, FALL ASLEEP WATCHING TV, AND STAGGER OFF TO BED WHERE YOU CAN HAVE NIGHTMARES ABOUT WORK

IT'S TWO OR THREE HOURS TILL QUITTING TIME. START WINDING DOWN, TIDYING UP YOUR DESK, STRETCHING, GABBING, AND THINKIN' ABOUT DINNER.
I'M HAVIN FISHSTICKS TONIGHT.   YUM!!

CONDUCT A SECRET LOVE AFFAIR WITH ONE OF YOUR CO-WORKERS, MAKING SURE YOU NEVER GET CAUGHT. WITHIN TWO WEEKS, REALIZE EVERYONE IN THE OFFICE KNOWS.

WORK—THE GAME

YOU CAN PLAY ALONE, OR WITH ANY NUMBER OF SO-CALLED FRIENDS.

YOU WILL NEED

PAIR O' DICE

A SMALL INSIGNIFICANT OBJECT TO REPRESENT YOU

RULES

TAKE TURNS GOING AROUND AND AROUND AND AROUND AND AROUND THE BOARD. THE OLDEST PLAYER ROLLS FIRST. THE RICHEST PLAYER STANDS BY, WATCHING AND LAUGHING.

CHEATING IS ENCOURAGED, BUT DON'T GET CAUGHT. YOU MAY SUFFER SEVERE PENALTIES.

PLAYING FAIR IS TOLERATED, BUT DON'T GET CAUGHT. YOU MAY SUFFER SEVERE PENALTIES.

THE GAME IS OVER WHEN YOU DIE.

BLAME SOMEONE ELSE FOR YOUR MISTAKES.
YOU SCREWED UP EVERYTHING AGAIN, STUPID!!

GET PARANOID

ARE THEY TRYING TO MAKE YOU MISERABLE SO YOU'LL GET FED UP AND QUIT?

START A PLOT AGAINST A CO-WORKER TO MAKE HIM OR HER SO PARANOID AND MISERABLE THAT HE OR SHE WILL GET FED UP AND QUIT.
DID YOU SEE THE PAPERS I LEFT ON THE XEROX MACHINE?
NOPE.

BECOME PARALYZED BY DISSATISFACTION, PESSIMISM, AND HOSTILITY
I HATE EVERYTHING.
THIS WORK IS POINTLESS.
WHY IS EVERYONE SO GRUMPY?

LAUGH WEAKLY AT ONE OF THE BOSS'S UNFUNNY JOKES.
THEN THEY ALL GOT AIDS AND DIED.
HA HA WHAT A KNEESLAPPER

LUNCH
TASTELESS SALAD AND SUGARLESS GUM, —OR— GREASY BURGER AND A COUPLE OF BEERS?

SPACE OUT FOR A FEW MINUTES.
SNAP BACK TO REALITY AND HOPE NO ONE HAS NOTICED.

USING ONLY SOME PUSHPINS AND AN ERASER, MAKE YOURSELF A LITTLE PIG!!!

AFFLICTION CORNER
CHOOSE ONE:
☐ HEADACHES.
☐ ULCERS.
☐ EXHAUSTION.
☐ DEPRESSION.
☐ VOICES IN YOUR HEAD.

IF YOU DRINK, DON'T DRILL

TITLE: LIFE IN HELL

AUTHOR: MATT GROENING © 1982*

HOW TO KILL 8 HOURS A DAY AND STILL KEEP YOUR JOB

*IF YOU XEROX THIS AND STICK IT ON THE OFFICE BULLETIN BOARD YOU'RE IN BIG TROUBLE.

IT AIN'T THAT EASY, BUT IF YOU'VE GOT AN AVERAGE MIND AND A VAGUE, ILL-DEFINED SENSE OF RESENTMENT, YOU SHOULD BE ABLE TO FOLLOW THIS EASY GUIDE AND GET AWAY WITH MURDER.

MINIMUM DAILY REQUIREMENTS
- ☐ A DESK SITUATED SO YOU CAN ESCAPE SCRUTINY.
- ☐ A WINDOW TO STARE OUT OF.
- ☐ A GOOD ACTING ABILITY.

IT'S ALWAYS TIME FOR A COFFEE BREAK!

STEPS!!!
CHECK TO SEE IF THERE'S ANY COFFEE BREWING.

MR. KOFFEEMEISTER

RETURN TO DESK AND GET CUP. RINSE OUT CUP. POUR COFFEE. BLOW ON IT. SIP SLOWLY.

WHAT TO HAVE WITH YOUR COFFEE
- ☐ NONDAIRY CREME POWDER
- ☐ ARTIFICIAL SWEETENER
- ☐ DONUT
- ☐ ANOTHER DONUT -- WHY THE HELL NOT?

COFFEE-BREAK PROJECTS

BORED?
WHY NOT:
- ○ XEROX YOUR HAND?
- ○ THINK ABOUT YESTERYEAR?
- ○ START VICIOUS RUMORS ABOUT A CO-WORKER?

→ WATCH GREASY FILM AT SURFACE OF COFFEE SWIRL AROUND. MAKE WEIRD PATTERNS IN STYROFOAM CUP WITH THUMBNAIL.

THINGS YOU CAN DO W/O MOVING A MUSCLE
WATCH THE CLOCK.
HUM TUNELESSLY.
DAYDREAM.
STARE INTO SPACE.
BLANK OUT.
STEW IN YOUR OWN JUICES.
TAKE A BREATHER.
SIGH.

3 QUESTIONS TO ASK YOURSELF
- • HAVE I CHECKED MY WORK?
- • HAVE I DOUBLE-CHECKED MY WORK?
- • HAVE I TRIPLE-CHECKED MY WORK?

MEMOS:
WRITE 'EM.
READ 'EM.
IGNORE 'EM.

NEVER
JUST WANDER AROUND. ALWAYS HAVE A PIECE OF PAPER IN YOUR HAND AND LOOK LIKE YOU'RE GOING SOMEWHERE.

HANDY PHRASES
"GOOOOOOD MORNING."
"WHAT A DAY!"
"OHH, MY BACK."
"HAVE A GOOD ONE."

PETTY BUT ODDLY SATISFYING OFFICE PRANKS
PUT ALL CALLERS ON HOLD FOREVER. PRESS ALL THE BUTTONS IN THE ELEVATOR. BORROW PENS AND NEVER RETURN THEM.

BE CREATIVE!

PAPER CLIP   BECOMES THIS   MODERN MINISCULPTURE

HANDY HINTS! E-Z & FUN!!
- ✓ CLIP FINGERNAILS.
- ✓ PAINT FINGERNAILS.
- ✓ BITE FINGERNAILS.
- ✓ SNIFF AT AIR.
- ✓ MEMORIZE CALORIE CHART.
- ✓ UNWRAP AND CHEW GUM.
- ✓ SWIVEL HEAD ON NECK.

FOR ADVANCED WORKERS ONLY:
HUNT AND KILL PESKY FLIES. MAKE AND SAIL PAPER AIRPLANES. KISS AND GROPE A CO-WORKER.

FOR A CHANGE OF PACE, ORGANIZE FREQUENT LITTLE OFFICE BIRTHDAY PARTIES!!

MAKE SURE EVERYONE ELSE IS JUST AS SLOW AS YOU ARE. A CONSISTENT WE'RE-ALL-IN-THIS-TOGETHER ATTITUDE CAN INSPIRE YOU ALL TO DEPTHS OF SLOTH AND INEFFICIENCY YOU NEVER KNEW EXISTED. IT'S EASY!!

FANTASIZE ABOUT HAVING SEX WITH EACH PERSON WHO WALKS THROUGH THE DOOR.

DON'T FORGET TO DOODLE!!!

UH OH! HERE COMES TROUBLE!

WHEN YOU GET CAUGHT:	YOU SAY:
SNOOPING	"I'M LOOKING FOR AN ERASER."
SLEEPING	"I'VE GOT IT!! A GREAT NEW IDEA FOR -- [THINK FAST]."
SHIRKING	"I THOUGHT I WAS S'POSED TO BE DOING THIS."

SMILE!!! ... THE KEY TO SUCCESS

MAKE YOUR OWN OFFICE TOYS

WITH PUSHPINS AND AN ERASER, YOU CAN MAKE A LITTLE PIG.

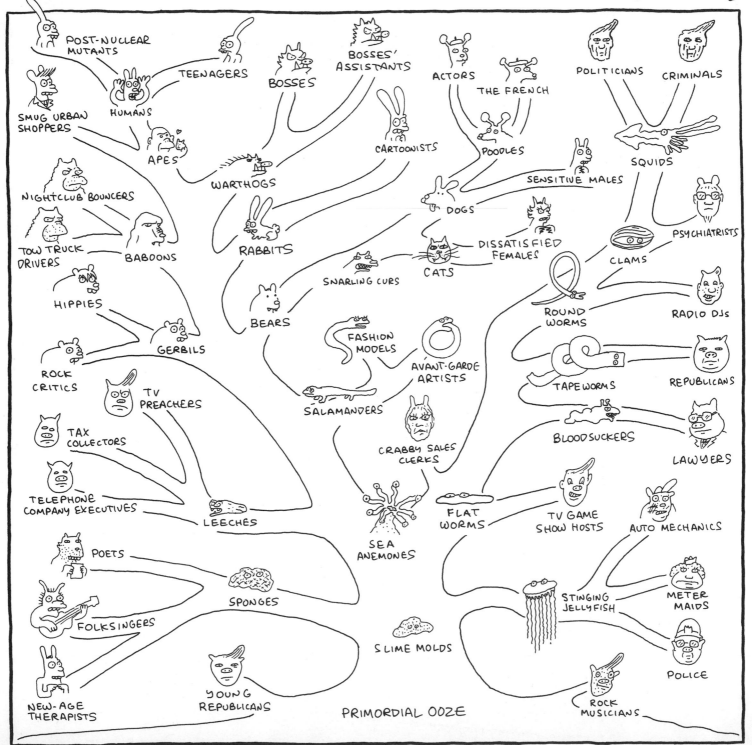

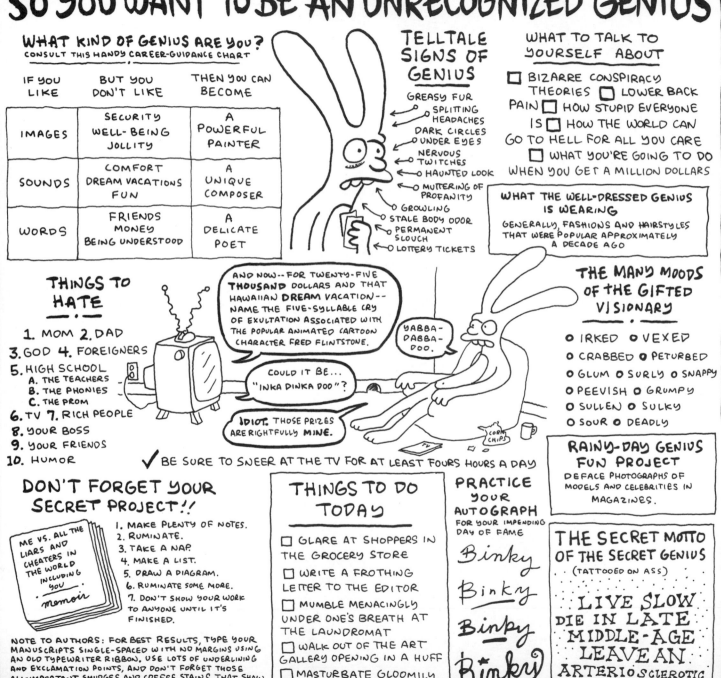

SO YOU WANT TO BE AN UNRECOGNIZED GENIUS

WHAT KIND OF GENIUS ARE YOU?
CONSULT THIS HANDY CAREER-GUIDANCE CHART

IF YOU LIKE	BUT YOU DON'T LIKE	THEN YOU CAN BECOME
IMAGES	SECURITY WELL-BEING JOLLITY	A POWERFUL PAINTER
SOUNDS	COMFORT DREAM VACATIONS FUN	A UNIQUE COMPOSER
WORDS	FRIENDS MONEY BEING UNDERSTOOD	A DELICATE POET

TELLTALE SIGNS OF GENIUS

- GREASY FUR
- SPLITTING HEADACHES
- DARK CIRCLES UNDER EYES
- NERVOUS TWITCHES
- HAUNTED LOOK
- MUTTERING OF PROFANITY
- GROWLING
- STALE BODY ODOR
- PERMANENT SLOUCH
- LOTTERY TICKETS

WHAT TO TALK TO YOURSELF ABOUT

- ☐ BIZARRE CONSPIRACY THEORIES
- ☐ LOWER BACK PAIN
- ☐ HOW STUPID EVERYONE IS
- ☐ HOW THE WORLD CAN GO TO HELL FOR ALL YOU CARE
- ☐ WHAT YOU'RE GOING TO DO WHEN YOU GET A MILLION DOLLARS

WHAT THE WELL-DRESSED GENIUS IS WEARING
GENERALLY, FASHIONS AND HAIRSTYLES THAT WERE POPULAR APPROXIMATELY A DECADE AGO

THINGS TO HATE
1. MOM 2. DAD
3. GOD 4. FOREIGNERS
5. HIGH SCHOOL
  A. THE TEACHERS
  B. THE PHONIES
  C. THE PROM
6. TV 7. RICH PEOPLE
8. YOUR BOSS
9. YOUR FRIENDS
10. HUMOR

AND NOW — FOR TWENTY-FIVE **THOUSAND** DOLLARS AND THAT HAWAIIAN **DREAM VACATION** — NAME THE FIVE-SYLLABLE CRY OF EXULTATION ASSOCIATED WITH THE POPULAR ANIMATED CARTOON CHARACTER FRED FLINTSTONE.

YABBA-DABBA-DOO.

COULD IT BE... "INKA DINKA DOO"?

IDIOT. THOSE PRIZES ARE RIGHTFULLY **MINE.**

✓ BE SURE TO SNEER AT THE TV FOR AT LEAST FOURS HOURS A DAY

THE MANY MOODS OF THE GIFTED VISIONARY

- ○ IRKED ○ VEXED
- ○ CRABBED ○ PETURBED
- ○ GLUM ○ SURLY ○ SNAPPY
- ○ PEEVISH ○ GRUMPY
- ○ SULLEN ○ SULKY
- ○ SOUR ○ DEADLY

RAINY-DAY GENIUS FUN PROJECT
DEFACE PHOTOGRAPHS OF MODELS AND CELEBRITIES IN MAGAZINES.

CORN CHIPS

DON'T FORGET YOUR SECRET PROJECT!!

ME VS. ALL THE LIARS AND CHEATERS IN THE WORLD INCLUDING YOU
memoir

1. MAKE PLENTY OF NOTES.
2. RUMINATE.
3. TAKE A NAP.
4. MAKE A LIST.
5. DRAW A DIAGRAM.
6. RUMINATE SOME MORE.
7. DON'T SHOW YOUR WORK TO ANYONE UNTIL IT'S FINISHED.

NOTE TO AUTHORS: FOR BEST RESULTS, TYPE YOUR MANUSCRIPTS SINGLE-SPACED WITH NO MARGINS USING AN OLD TYPEWRITER RIBBON, USE LOTS OF UNDERLINING AND EXCLAMATION POINTS, AND DON'T FORGET THOSE ALL-IMPORTANT SMUDGES AND COFFEE STAINS THAT SHOW THE CONSUMING INTENSITY OF YOUR INNER TORMENT.

THINGS TO DO TODAY
- ☐ GLARE AT SHOPPERS IN THE GROCERY STORE
- ☐ WRITE A FROTHING LETTER TO THE EDITOR
- ☐ MUMBLE MENACINGLY UNDER ONE'S BREATH AT THE LAUNDROMAT
- ☐ WALK OUT OF THE ART GALLERY OPENING IN A HUFF
- ☐ MASTURBATE GLOOMILY

PRACTICE YOUR AUTOGRAPH
FOR YOUR IMPENDING DAY OF FAME

Binky
Binky
Binky
Binky

THE SECRET MOTTO OF THE SECRET GENIUS
(TATTOOED ON ASS)

LIVE SLOW DIE IN LATE MIDDLE-AGE LEAVE AN ARTERIOSCLEROTIC CORPSE

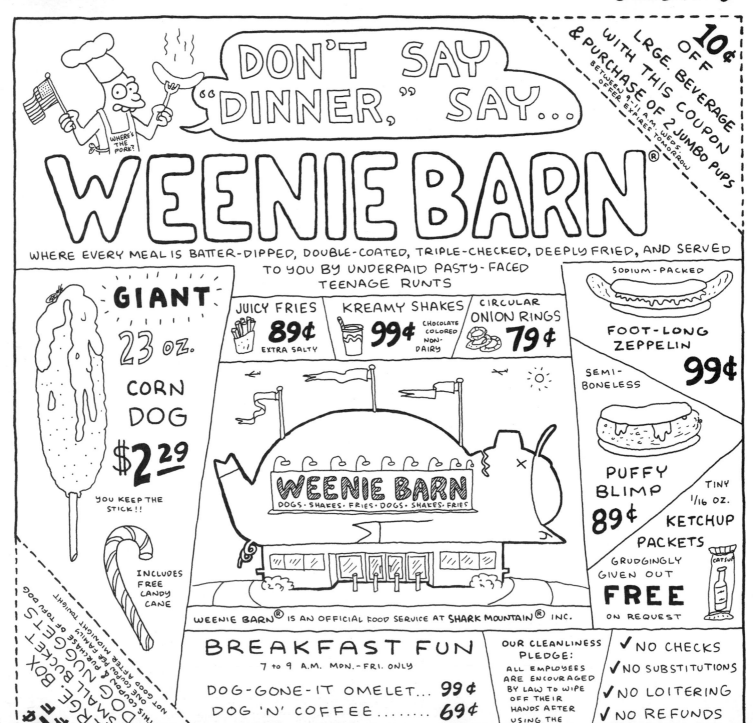

LIFE IN HELL

WHAT WILL YOU SAY ON YOUR DEATHBED?

ZZZZ ZZ ZZZZ

YOU FOLLOW THIS GUIDE AND THEY WILL RARELY EVER CALL YOU

SLEEPYHEAD

AGAIN.

IS THIS YOU?

RRRRRRRRBNNNNNNNNNGGO

TIRED OF HEARING THE SAME OLD THING?

"HI, GROGGY."

"HEY, LAZYBONES."

"YO, PUFFY."

"YOU'RE FIRED."

WELL, REMEMBER:

THE EARLY BIRD GETS ALL THE SQUIRMING, WRIGGLY MEALWORMS.

JUST FOLLOW THIS SIMPLE 9-POINT RISE-'N'-SHINE WAKE-UP PLAN AND WE'LL HAVE YOU ON YOUR FEET IN ~~NO TIME~~ LESS THAN AN HOUR.

GET AT LEAST 2 OR 3 HOURS OF SLEEP A NIGHT. TRY NOT TO GO TO BED DRUNK OR WITH EXCITABLE STRANGERS.

WHAT'S FER BREAKFAST?

GET MOVING.

YEAH YEAH YEAH--YOU DON'T WANT TO GET UP IN THE MORNING. TELL ME ABOUT IT, SNOOZY. YOU GOT IT EASY. SOME PEOPLE HAVE TO BE OUT OF BED BY 9 A.M. THREE OR FOUR DAYS A WEEK.

COUNT YOUR BLESSINGS.

SET THREE CLOCKS WITH PAINFULLY SHRILL AND PIERCING ALARMS THAT WON'T QUIT OUT OF ARM'S REACH.*

RRRRRBNNNNNGG RRRRRRRRNGGGG

WHIMPER

*TECHNIQUE COURTESY OF LYNDA J. BARRY

THE NEXT MOMENT IS **CRUCIAL.** IGNORE EVERYTHING YOUR BRAIN AND BODY TELL YOU, AND STUMBLE, STAGGER, OR CRAWL TO THE KITCHEN. AND NOW, YOUR REWARD.

A HOT THICK POTENT BITTER STEAMING MUG OF COFFEE.

YUM.

BREAKFAST DONUTS OPTIONAL.

NOW

YOU ARE AWAKE, FULLY REFRESHED, AND RARIN' TO GO.

JUST PRACTICE THESE TRADITIONAL UP-AND-AT-'EM GREETINGS:

"BEAUTIFUL DAY, ISN'T IT?"

"TOP O' THE MORNIN' TO YA."

"GET THE **HELL** OUTTA MY WAY."

ISN'T IT ABOUT TIME YOU QUIT YOUR LOUSY JOB?

I'M SORRY, I MUSTA BEEN DAYDREAMING. COULD YOU REPEAT THE QUESTION?

WAKE UP, CHUMPLY, YOU'RE NOT GETTING ANY YOUNGER. THE CLOCK IS TICKING. YOU CAN'T JUST SIT THERE IN YOUR CUBBYHOLE WHILE LIFE PASSES YOU BY. YOU'RE WASTING YOUR VALUABLE TIME. YOU'VE GOT SYMPHONIES TO COMPOSE. NOVELS TO WRITE. SNOWMOBILES TO PURCHASE. LET'S GET OUR BUTTS IN GEAR RIGHT NOW.

I'VE GOT MY EYE ON YOU.

YOU WON'T MISS YOUR OLD BOSS, MOST LIKELY.

YOU CAN DO IT. YOU CAN DO IT. YOU CAN DO IT. YOU CAN DO IT. YOU CAN DO IT. YOU MIGHT BE ABLE TO DO IT. MAYBE.

JUST THINK: NO MORE WAXY PASTRIES DURING YOUR COFFEE BREAK.

NO MORE MINDLESS CLOCK-WATCHING.

ASK NOT FOR WHOM THE OVERHEAD FLUORESCENT LIGHTING HUMS.

NO MORE SENSELESS PRATTLE WITH YOUR COWORKERS.

NO MORE POINTLESS GROVELING.

ANYBODY SEE NEWHART LAST NIGHT? WOTTA SCREAM.

SOMEDAY I HOPE TO DIRECT.

THESE TWO FAGS WALK INTO A BAR

WHAT? OF COURSE I LIKE WORKING HERE, SIR.

YES, SIR.

YES, SIR.

RIGHT AWAY, SIR.

THE MOMENT OF JOY

I QUIT. I QUIT. I QUIT.

PEACE OF MIND

MOVING RIGHT ALONG

ISN'T IT ABOUT TIME I GET ANOTHER LOUSY JOB?

HOW TO KILL 6 HOURS A DAY, 5 DAYS A WEEK, 9 MONTHS A YEAR, TILL YOU'RE 18 YEARS OLD

IT AIN'T GONNA BE EASY, BUT LOOK AT IT THIS WAY: YOU GET LOTS OF PRACTICE.

SOME FUN!

MAKE GROTESQUE FACES WHEN THE TEACHER ISN'T LOOKING. ALSO WEIRD MARTIAN NOISES.

GEEBA GEEBA

SCATTER BALL BEARINGS ON THE FLOOR.

FIND STRAY DOGS AND PUT 'EM IN THE COAT CLOSET.

Learn to mew like a kitten without moving your lips. Drives teachers crazy.

DID YOU KNOW?

FLINGING SLICED BEETS UPWARD WILL OFTEN CAUSE THEM TO ADHERE TO THE CAFETERIA CEILING.

HOW TO KEEP YOUR BRAIN ALIVE IN SCHOOL: DRAW.

✓ IN YOUR NOTEBOOK. ✓ IN YOUR TEXTBOOK. ✓ ON YOUR DESK.

WHAT TO DRAW: HORSES. MONSTERS. ROCKETSHIPS. DINOSAURS. WARS. MAZES. CARS. CITIES OF THE FUTURE. VOLCANOES. MESSY SCRIBBLES.

ONLY 13 YEARS TO GO.

IMMATURE!

HIDE THE BLACKBOARD ERASERS IN THE CLASS KISS-ASS'S DESK.

PUT GARDEN SLUGS IN THE DRINKING FOUNTAINS.

EEK

MAKE UP YOUR OWN WORDS DURING THE PLEDGE OF ALLEGIANCE.

I PLUCK ALUMINUM FROM THE FACE OF THE YOU-KNOW-WHATS OF AMNESIA

SPECIAL PROJECT

YOU CAN MAKE A USELESS TEXTBOOK BEARABLE BY DRAWING MOUSTACHES AND BLACKING OUT TEETH IN EVERY PICTURE.

ESSENTIAL WEAPONRY

TINY SQUIRT GUN

WATER BALLOONS

RUBBER BANDS

CAFETERIA FOOD

WHATEVER YOU DO

DON'T GET PREGNANT. DON'T GET ANYONE ELSE PREGNANT.

FOR YOUR INFORMATION
* YOU'RE NOT GOING TO GO TO HELL.
* YES, BEING AN ADULT IS A DRAG, BUT THE ORGASMS ARE TERRIFIC.

IN GENERAL

DISTRACT YOUR FRIENDS. GIGGLE MORONICALLY. PASS NOTES. WHISPER. DOODLE. DAYDREAM. LOOK OUT THE WINDOW. DON'T GET CAUGHT.

WARNING TO YOUNG CONSUMERS: X-RAY SPEX DON'T WORK.

REMEMBER, WHEN YOU'RE REALLY GOING CRAZY:

YOU CAN SKIP SCHOOL OCCASIONALLY.

COMICS

READ 'EM. DRAW 'EM. TRADE 'EM.

WHEN YOU FINALLY ESCAPE FROM SCHOOL

DON'T GET MARRIED RIGHT AWAY.

DON'T JOIN THE ARMY.

DON'T GET MARRIED RIGHT AWAY AND HAVE A MESS OF BABIES.

DON'T BORE KIDS OR BE MEAN TO THEM.

LIFE IN HELL

WHY DON'T YOU QUIT YOUR JOB RIGHT NOW AND GO INTO BUSINESS FOR YOURSELF?

© 1982 BY MATT GROENING

DON'T READ THIS **NOW**, YOU FOOL-- YOU WANT TO GET FIRED? WAIT TILL YOUR LUNCHBREAK SO YOU CAN GET AWAY FROM **PRYING EYES**.

OKAY. NOW THAT WE HAVE SOME PRIVACY, LET'S BE FRANK. YOU'RE FED UP, AREN'T YOU? **JEEZ, CALM DOWN, WILLYA?** YOU DON'T HAVE TO SCREAM.

AND YOU COULD BE THAT NUDE LAUGHING GUY [OR GAL] -- YOU KNOW YOU COULD -- IF YOU'D JUST QUIT YOUR BELLYACHING AND GET OFF YOUR DUFF.

IT WON'T BE EASY -- DON'T KID YOURSELF -- BUT YOU'VE GOT TO DECIDE **RIGHT NOW** THAT THIS IS **IT** -- NO IFS, ANDS, OR BUTS.

THIS FREEDOM STUFF IS **SCARY**, HUH? ESPECIALLY FOR YOU, WITH ALL YOUR FINANCIAL AND SOCIAL RESPONSIBILITIES. BUT DON'T WAVER NOW -- THIS IS YOUR **BIG CHANCE.**

CHOMP SLURP

SURE IT'S TOUGH OUT THERE. BUT THE LONGER YOU WAIT THE TOUGHER IT GETS. UH OH. LUNCHTIME IS ALMOST OVER.

I CAN TELL. THAT LOOK IN YOUR EYES -- THE WAY YOU STEW AND STEAM -- THAT GNASHING OF TEETH -- YOUR COMPULSIVE SNACKING. IT ALL FITS.

YOU SIMPLY DON'T LIKE YOUR CRAPPY JOB OR YOUR MINISCULE SALARY OR YOUR TYRANNICAL BOSS OR YOUR PALTRY FRINGE BENEFITS OR YOUR LACK OF PRESTIGE OR YOUR MEANINGLESS DUTIES OR YOUR HAVING TO GET UP EARLY IN THE MORNING.

FIRST THING YOU'VE GOT TO DO IS TAKE STOCK OF YOURSELF. DO I HAVE WHAT IT TAKES? CAN I STAND UP FOR MYSELF? HAVE I SALTED AWAY TWENTY GRAND IN A SECRET BANK ACCOUNT?

DON'T DESPAIR. YOU CAN DO IT. FAR BETTER TO BE FREE THAN A SLAVE, RIGHT? THINK POSITIVE. THINK OF THOSE BASTARDS YOU'LL BE LEAVING BEHIND FOREVER.

WHAT'S IT GOING TO BE -- AUTONOMY OR DRUDGERY? BLINDING HEADACHES OR ALL THE SNOOZING YOU CAN TAKE?

HURRY UP AND DECIDE. YOU'VE GOT JUST A COUPLE MINUTES LEFT. YOU CAN DO IT. YOU CAN. WELL? C'MON....

AND YOU KNOW SOMETHING? YOU'RE NOT ALONE. BUT THE DIFFERENCE BETWEEN YOU AND THEM IS YOU'RE STILL STUCK IN A RUT, WHILE ALL THOSE OTHERS HAVE ALREADY ESCAPED INTO LIVES OF ADVENTURE, FUN, AND BIG PAY.

REMEMBER THAT GUY, WHATSISNAME, WHO WORKED HERE FOR ABOUT SIX MONTHS, THEN HE SUDDENLY QUIT? WELL THAT GUY IS LYING NUDE IN A HAMMOCK IN SUNNY BALI RIGHT NOW, SIPPING ON COCONUT MILK AND **LAUGHING** AT YOU.

BE YOUR OWN BOSS. GO INTO BUSINESS FOR YOURSELF. BE CREATIVE. BE TALENTED. APPLY YOURSELF. CREATE SEVERAL MASTERPIECES. IT'S NOT AS HARD AS IT LOOKS.

HUNT FOR DROPPED WALLETS ON THE SIDE-WALK. GO FISHING WITH A POWERFUL MAGNET. LICK ENVELOPES AT HOME IN YOUR SPARE TIME. PRAY TO GOD FOR BETTER LUCK. ACT SINCERE.

YEAH, THAT'S A GOOD IDEA. **THINK ABOUT IT.** WAIT TILL AFTER PAYDAY. WHAT'S THE RUSH? YOU'VE BEEN HERE __ YEARS ALREADY, ANYWAY. MUST'N'T BE TOO HASTY.

OOPS, GOTTA RUN. BOSS'S GONNA **KILL** ME. BYE!! SEE YA TOMORROW!!

LIFE IN HELL
©1986 BY MATT GROENING
GRAND REOPENING NOW UNDER NEW MANAGERS
PLENTY SUDS
AKBAR 'N' JEFF'S LAUNDRO-HUT
FREE LINT
WASH & FUN
U WASH
U DRY
U WAIT
U SCRAM
NOT RESPONSIBLE FOR LOSS OR DAMAGE
NO SOMOS RESPONSABLES POR PERDIDA O DAÑOS
BUBBLE ACTION
DANGER
DO NOT CLIMB IN, ON, AROUND, OR BEHIND MACHINES
25 WASHERS
3 BIG DRYERS
1 COMFY BENCH
COINS GALORE IN OUR CHANGE MACHINE
SORRY NO REFUNDS
LAUNDRO-HUT RULES AND REGULATIONS
1. MACHINES ARE FOR CLOTHES ONLY -- NO PETS, TOYS, INFLATABLE BOATS, INFLATABLE DOLLS, CONDOMS, OR TIRES CAN BE ALLOWED.
2. DERISIVE COMMENTS ABOUT THE UNDERGARMENTS OF OTHER CUSTOMERS MAY RESULT IN SERIOUS INJURY OR DEATH.
3. DO NOT PLACE INFANTS IN EMPTY MACHINES TO KEEP THEM FROM RUNNING AROUND.
4. NO "SAVING" WASHERS AND DRYERS SOLELY FOR CUSTOMERS OF YOUR OWN ETHNIC GROUP.
5. SUICIDES ARE NO LONGER ALLOWED ON THE PREMISES.
PRESENT THIS AD FOR FREE STRAY SOCK
LIMIT 1 PER FAMILY PER VISIT
NO PURCHASE NECESSARY
FLUFFY-KLEEN® AND STROFTY-BRITE® ARE REGISTERED TRADEMARKS OF JEF-BAR-CO, INC.
ALL RIGHTS RESERVED
"NOT ALL THAT DEPRESSING"
LOCATED ACROSS THE STREET FROM THE OLD MALL BETWEEN AKBAR & JEFF'S TOFU HUT AND BINKY'S TANNING BARN

PARENTS' GUIDE TO TEENAGE CRIME & PUNISHMENT

THE PROBLEM	THE CRIME	THE RESPONSE	THE PUNISHMENT	THE RESULT
"SCHOOL SUCKS"	SOME SMARTASS REMARK AT DINNER	ICY STARE — FORK POINTED IN KID'S DIRECTION "SHUT UP, YOU."	SILENT TREATMENT — BARELY PERCEPTIBLE SHAKING OF HEAD WHENEVER KID SPEAKS	KID WILL MOVE OUT AT 18, GET A JOB IN COMPUTER PROGRAMMING, BE MARRIED, MISERABLE, AND DIVORCED BY 23
"IT WAS JUST SOME CRUMMY OLD NECKLACES"	CAUGHT SHOPLIFTING DOWN AT THE MALL	SLOW SHAKING OF HEAD IN DISGUST "SO YOU'RE A SLIMY LITTLE THIEF. I HOPE YOU'RE PROUD OF YOURSELF."	NO ALLOWANCE 2 MOS. GROUNDED 1 MO. REPROACHFUL LOOKS FROM NOW ON	KID WILL GO TO COMMUNITY COLLEGE, DROP OUT AFTER 2½ SEMESTERS, GO TO WORK FOR DAD'S BUSINESS
"HI DAD"	INSOLENT HAIR AND CLOTHING	SNORTS OF DISBELIEF "YOU'RE NOT LEAVING THIS HOUSE TILL YOU LOOK DECENT."	CONFISCATE CLOTHING CONTINUOUS BELITTLING SHIP KID OFF TO MILITARY SCHOOL	KID WILL SHAPE UP UPON GRADUATION, JOIN ARMY, WOUND SELF ON PATROL IN CENTRAL AMERICA
"AW, WE'RE JUST PLAYIN 'TWISTER'"	HEAVY PETTING OR WORSE WITH SOME SQUINTY LITTLE CREEP IN THE BASEMENT REC ROOM	"JUST WHAT IN GOD'S NAME IS GOING ON AROUND HERE?"	KID'S DATE BANISHED EARLY CURFEW COMPULSORY CHURCH ATTENDANCE	KID WILL RUN AWAY AT 16, HITCHHIKE TO NEXT STATE, GET A JOB IN A TIRE WAREHOUSE, SETTLE DOWN BY 18
"THAT'S MY LITTLE RUBBER EAR WARMER"	SECRET INSPECTION OF BEDROOM REVEALS BIRTH CONTROL PILLS OR DEVICES	FLARING NOSTRILS HUFFING AND PUFFING SPUTTERING MAYBE KNOCK THE KID AROUND A BIT	EARLY CURFEW GROUNDED 1 MO. CONTINUED SECRET INSPECTIONS OF BEDROOM GLOWERING LOOKS	KID WILL BE MARRIED BY 19, 2 KIDS BY 21, 3 KIDS BY 23, COMPLETELY DEMORALIZED BY 25
"I ONLY PUT IT IN A LITTLE" / "WE'RE IN LOVE"	PREGNANT	"HOW THE **HELL** DID YOU GET PREGNANT?"	KICK KID OUT OF THE HOUSE	BABY WILL BE ABORTED OR GIVEN UP FOR ADOPTION, KID WILL MOVE ACROSS COUNTRY AND NEVER SPEAK TO YOU AGAIN
"I'M HOME" / "WOO"	HOME AFTER CURFEW BEER ON BREATH	"IF THERE'S **ONE** SCRATCH ON MY CAR, YOU'RE GOING TO WISH YOU WERE NEVER BORN."	NO BORROWING DAD'S CAR 2 MOS. EARLY CURFEW BALEFUL LOOKS	KID WILL GO TO COLLEGE, JOIN FRATERNITY OR SORORITY, MEET FUTURE SPOUSE, GET MARRIED, END UP JUST LIKE YOU

LIFE IN HELL

LAST-MINUTE GIFT SUGGESTIONS UNDER $5

JAR O' GRAVEL

ONLY 39¢

ORIGAMI BOULDERS

LESS THAN 2¢ EACH!!

NAPKIN DISPENSER

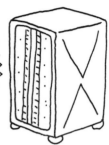

FREE WITH MEAL AT RESTAURANTS (WEAR BULKY OVERCOAT)

LITTLE PIG MADE OUT OF AN ERASER AND SOME PUSHPINS

FREE

(GET MATERIALS AT OFFICE WHERE YOU WORK)

GARAGE SALE AND LOST PET SIGNS

YARD SALE SAT 10-5 AROUND CORNER

CAT MISSING HAVE YOU SEEN STINKY? CALL 655-881#

COMICAL BAR NAPKINS

FREE WITH DRINK

"I'M BORED." ZIP

DO-IT-YOURSELF CELEBRITY AUTOGRAPH

Chubby Checker

SAME PRICE AS ORIGAMI BOULDERS!

LOOSE CHANGE

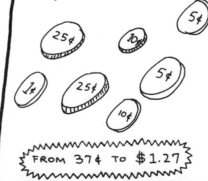

FROM 37¢ TO $1.27

JAR O' LEAVES

MERELY 39¢

AND REMEMBER: YOU CAN WRAP ALL YOUR GIFTS IN THE GAILY COLORED PAGES OF THIS PUBLICATION.

LIFE IN HELL
©1986 BY MATT GROENING
THE ROAD TO MANHOOD
FIRST SAFETY-PIN JAB DURING DIAPER CHANGE
FIRST WEANING
GOO
FIRST STEP
FIRST FALL
FIRST PEEK UP TEACHER'S DRESS WHILE LYING ON FLOOR DURING NAP-TIME AT NURSERY SCHOOL
FIRST LECTURE THAT PENIS "IS NOT A TOY"
I SWEAR TO GOD I DIDN'T DO IT.
SHE DID.
FIRST LIE TOLD TO ESCAPE PUNISHMENT
THERE WAS THIS LADY AND SHE HAD THIS LITTLE DOG AND THE LITTLE DOG'S NAME WAS "FREESHOW."
FIRST DIRTY JOKE HEARD
AND SO THE LITTLE DOG JUMPED OUT THE WINDOW AND THE NAKED LADY RAN DOWN THE STREET AFTER HIM, YELLING "FREESHOW! FREESHOW!"
HA HA HA
FIRST DIRTY JOKE UNDERSTOOD
FIRST PROFANITY OVERHEARD BY PARENT
FIRST VICTIMIZATION BY BIGGER, OLDER KID
FIRST VICTIMIZATION OF SMALLER, YOUNGER KID
FIRST 10,000 HOURS OF WATCHING TV
FIRST REALIZATION THAT GIRLS MIGHT NOT BE THE ENEMY
CATCH 22
FIRST REALIZATION THAT EVERYTHING YOU'VE BEEN TAUGHT IS A LIE
FIRST COMPULSIVE MASTURBATION
FIRST TIME DRUNK
FIRST CAR ACCIDENT
FIRST FURTIVE SEXUAL EXPERIENCE
FIRST SEXUALLY TRANSMITTED DISEASE
FIRST MARRIAGE
FIRST DIVORCE
FIRST TAX AUDIT
FIRST REALIZATION YOU MIGHT NOT WRITE THE GREAT AMERICAN NOVEL BEFORE YOU'RE THIRTY
FIRST REALIZATION YOU MUST BE A MAN, 'CAUSE YOU'RE NOT A KID ANYMORE

Life in Hell

THE MASSAGE

IT'S LIKE A PARTY SOMETIMES IT MAKES ME WONDER HOW I KEEP MYSELF SO SLENDER. IT'S LIKE A PARTY SOMETIMES IT MAKES ME WONDER HOW I KEEP MYSELF SO SLENDER.

BROKEN HEARTS EVERYWHERE, HERPES INNA HOT TUB YOU KNOW THEY JUST DON'T CARE. I CAN'T TAKE THE SMOG, CAN'T TAKE THE HEAT, BUT I DIG PICK 'N' SAVE YOU KNOW THEIR PRICES CAN'T BE BEAT. DOG CRAP IN THE FRONT YARD, HIBACHI'S IN THE BACK, JUNIOR'S IN THE DRIVEWAY WITH A BIG MAC ATTACK. I TRIED TO TAKE LUNCH BUT I COULDN'T LEAVE HOME, 'CAUSE THE MAN FROM THE CAR SHOP IS SHINING MY CHROME.

DON'T PUSH ME 'CAUSE I'M CLOSE TO THE EDGE OF THE POOL. IT'S LIKE A PARTY SOMETIMES IT MAKES ME WONDER HOW I KEEP MYSELF SO SLENDER. YOU SHOVE ME IN AND I'M GONNA LOSE MY COOL.

MY SON SAID POPS I DON'T WANNA GO TO CLASS, 'CAUSE I'M FUNCTIONALLY ILLITERATE BUT STILL I'LL PASS. LIFE IS A BREEZE, I'M GONNA WAX MY SKIS, EMPTY YOUR POCKETS 'CAUSE I NEED YOUR KEYS. YOU KNOW WHAT'S FUNNY? I'M GONNA INHERIT ALL YOUR MONEY. NOW EAT YOUR BRIE BEFORE IT GETS TOO RUNNY. I'M NOT A SLAVE, I DIG NEW WAVE, I'M GONNA DANCE TO THE GO-GOS ON YOUR GRAVE.

DON'T PUSH ME UNLESS YOU'VE GOT A LOT 'CAUSE I'LL SUE YOU FOR EVERYTHING YOU GOT. IT'S LIKE A PARTY SOMETIMES IT MAKES ME WONDER HOW I KEEP MYSELF SO SLENDER.

A KID IS BORN WITH A WHACK ON THE BUTT, IF A BOY RIGHT AWAY THEN HIS PENIS IS CUT. THEN THERE'S GOD UP ABOVE AND HE'S BEAMING DOWN LOVE, 'CEPT WHEN HE'S FRISKY THEN HE GIVES YOU A SHOVE. YOU GROW UP IN THE SUBURBS LIVING FIRST RATE, WHEN YOUR PARENTS AREN'T HOME YOU GET TO STAY UP LATE. THE MALL WHERE YOU SHOP AND YOUR HOMEGROWN CROP MAKE YOU FEEL SURE YOU'RE GONNA STAY ON TOP. WHEN YOUR FOLKS CALL YOU LIAR YOU'LL ASPIRE TO GET HIGHER. MAYBE IN FRUSTRATION YOU'LL GO PUNCTURE A TIRE. DRIVING DAD'S CAR, SPENDING TWENTIES AND TENS, LIFE IS A BALL AND YOU'RE UP ON THE TRENDS.

DON'T PUSH ME 'CAUSE I'M STANDING IN LINE. HERE-- CALM DOWN -- HAVE A SIP OF WINE. IT'S LIKE A PARTY SOMETIMES IT MAKES ME WONDER HOW I KEEP MYSELF SO SLENDER.

YOU SAY I'M COOL, I'M NO FOOL, BUT THEN YOU WIND UP APPLYING TO GRAD SCHOOL. NOW YOU'RE WORKING LIKE MAD, YOU'RE DRESSED IN PLAID, YOU DRIVE TO YOUR PAD IN YOUR VERY OWN CAD. YOUR BLANKET'S ELECTRIC, YOUR KID IS DYSLEXIC, YOU SAVE ON THE FOOD 'CAUSE YOUR WIFE'S ANORECTIC. YOU'RE A WHEELER-DEALER, ON THE BEACH YOU'RE A PEELER, IN THE WINTER YOU'RE A GUNG-HO SNOWMOBILER. YOU'VE GOT A FINE EDUCATION, A FINE CABLE STATION, AND EVERY YEAR YOU GET A FINE PAID VACATION. YOU'VE GOTTEN MATURE, YOU SAY "FER SURE," YOU BUY A FUR AND LISTEN TO YOUR WIFE PURR. AND WHEN IT'S OVER, AND YOU'RE DEAD OF CANCER, THEY'LL REMEMBER YOU FONDLY AS A DISCO DANCER. IT'S PLAIN TO SEE YOUR LIFE WAS FULL, A LITTLE ON THE LIGHT SIDE BUT NOT TOO DULL. AND NOW YOU'RE BURIED SIX FEET DEEP, SO YOU OPEN YOUR EYES FROM A VERY LONG SLEEP. YOU KNOW YOU'RE GONE AND YOU WONDER WELL, WHAT'S IT GONNA BE, HEAVEN OR HELL? BUT GOD'S A GUY WHO ACTS REAL SLY, HE'LL THINK UP SOMETHING WEIRD JUST TO GIVE IT A TRY. GOD'S A MAN WITH A PLAN WHO DOES WHAT HE CAN, SO YOU GOTTA HAVE FAITH AND TRY TO UNDERSTAND.

DON'T PUSH ME 'CAUSE I'M CLOSE TO THE EDGE. I'VE BEEN REINCARNATED AS A VERY SMALL TRIMMED HEDGE. IT'S LIKE A PARTY SOMETIMES IT MAKES ME WONDER HOW I KEEP MYSELF SO SLENDER.

LIFE IN HELL
PO BOX 36E64
LOS ANGELES CA 90036

YOU'VE TRIED THE REST, NOW TRY

SORRY, NO REFUNDS.

AKBAR & JEFF'S VIDEO HUT

—FORMERLY AKBAR & JEFF'S TOFU HUT—

ACROSS THE STREET FROM THE OLD MALL BETWEEN WUBBY'S RUB-A-DUB HOT TUBS AND THE COOKIE BARN

AS LOW AS 99¢ PER TAPE PER DAY WITH MEMBERSHIP IN VIDEO HUT FUN CLUB ($30) AND RENTAL OF 4 OTHER TAPES AT REGULAR PRICES

ALL THE LATEST SEQUELS IN EVERY CATEGORY!!!

TEENAGE SLASHER PIX!!

TEENAGE SEX COMEDIES!!

TEENAGE ACTION DRAMAS!!

TEENAGE ACTION COMEDIES!!

TEENAGE SEX DRAMAS!!

— AND MANY, MANY MORE —

HOME SWEET HOME

ICE CREAM

THIS COULD BE YOU!!!

DON'T FORGET OUR DISCREETLY SIZZLING HOT 'N' HORNY ADULT XXX-RATED VIDEO SHELF (MATURE THEMES)

➪ YOU MUST BE AT LEAST 18 AND HAVE NO SHAME

NEW!!

☆ THE FUZZ NUZZLERS
☆ THE SCUZZ GOBBLERS
☆ THE SLEAZE WHEEDLERS
☆ THE WHIZ DIDDLERS
☆ WALT DISNEY'S BEAVER VALLEY

CHECK OUT OUR KIDDIE KORNER

YAY

JUST IN:

EMPTY TAPE BOXES ARE ARRANGED IN SEMI-ALPHABETICAL ORDER FOR YOUR SHOPPING CONVENIENCE

YES, WE HAVE FOREIGN FILMS!!!!
• FIVE FLAMING KUNG-FU FINGERS OF DEATH
• SNØG BØGGEN (SWEDISH VERSION OF "FROSTY THE SNOWMAN")
• AN AMERICAN IN PARIS
+7 MORE!!

★ THE LITTLE BEAR WHO ITCHED
★ PUFFY & DROOLY KARTOONIVAL KLASSIX, VOL. 5
★ ANIMAL FARM
★ BONGO'S XMAS WISH

WARNING: CUSTOMERS CAUGHT TAPING OTHER MATERIAL OVER OUR MOVIES IN ORDER TO ANNOY THE NEXT PERSON WHO RENTS THE TAPE WILL BE PROSECUTED TO THE FULLEST EXTENT OF THE LAW

STAYING AT HOME WATCHING RENTED MOVIES ON TV IS YOUR SAFEST ENTERTAINMENT VALUE

LIFE IN HELL

LIFE IN HELL THEATRE PROUDLY PRESENTS

AKBAR & JEFF *in*

"AN OVERHEARD CONVERSATION"

DURING BREAKFAST AT A BEACH CAFE IN SUNNY CALIFORNIA 12/31/85

TONIGHT'S THE NIGHT.

THE BIG NIGHT.

THE **BIG** NIGHT.

NEW YEAR'S EVE.

SO WHERE'S THE PARTY?

IN VENICE.

VENICE?

YEP.

UGH.

LOTTA CHICKS IN VENICE.

YEAH?

EASY PICKINS.

YEAH?

WE COULD GET LUCKY.

YEAH?

FISH IN A BARREL.

WHAT?

I GOT THIS IDEA FOR A BUMPERSTICKER.

I REMEMBER NEW YEAR'S EVE IN PUERTO VALLARTA.

LISTEN.

WHAT A NIGHT.

IT GOES, "IF YOU DRINK, DON'T DRIVE-- YOU MIGHT HIT A BUMP AND SPILL YOUR DRINK."

YOU WOULDN'TA **BELIEVED** THIS HOTEL.

"HIT A BUMP AND SPILL YOUR DRINK."

WE COULD WEAR IT ON OUR T-SHIRTS. TO THE PARTY.

ALL THE ACCOMMODATIONS. ROOM SERVICE. **THREE** BARS. A SOLID MARBLE BALCONY THE SIZE OF A SWIMMING POOL.

WE COULD WEAR IT UNDER OUR CLOTHES.

AND YOU KNOW WHO WAS THERE? THAT NIGHT? IN THE HOTEL?

ROD STEWART.

ROD STEWART.

A BABE ON EACH ARM.

GUY KNOWS HOW TO LIVE.

HI! WHAT CAN I GET FOR YOU THIS MORNING?

COFFEE.

COFFEE. HOWDJA LIKE TO COME TO A PARTY TONIGHT?

NO THANKS. I'M STAYING HOME TONIGHT.

BUT IT'S NEW YEAR'S EVE!

I KNOW, BUT IT'S JUST NOT THE SAME. I'M FROM SYRACUSE, NEW YORK, AND EVERY NEW YEAR'S EVE, EVERYONE IN TOWN HEADS FOR THE HOTEL SYRACUSE.

THEY HAVE ALL THESE BALLROOMS OPEN, ALL THIS DANCING, AND IT'S JUST SO BEAUTIFUL, EVERY YEAR.

WHY ARE WE HERE?

GOOD QUESTION.

WHY ARE WE HERE?

WE SHOULD GO TO SYRACUSE.

PUERTO VALLARTA.

NEXT YEAR.

WHY ARE WE HERE?

DID I TELL YOU ABOUT MY STRANGE DREAM? I WAS IN THE DARK, I DON'T KNOW WHERE, AND I WAS LIKE STRUGGLING, STRUGGLING IN THE DARK, YOU KNOW?

AND MY HANDS WERE AROUND THIS, I WAS STRANGLING-- STRANGLING SOMEONE, I COULDN'T SEE WHO. AND YOU KNOW WHAT?

WHAT?

THE GUY I WAS STRANGLING WAS YOU.

I'VE STRANGLED **YOU** LOTS OF TIMES IN MY DREAMS.

LIFE IN HELL
©1986 BY MATT GROENING
THE ROAD TO WOMANHOOD
CONSULTATION BY
DEBORAH CAPLAN
MARGY ROCHLIN
SARAH RUKEYSER
MILI SMYTHE
ANN SUMMA
FIRST PIXIE CUT
FIRST TIME CROSSING THE STREET WITHOUT HOLDING MOM'S HAND
FIRST BARBIE
FIRST MAJOR BARBIE ACCESSORY*
* SUCH AS BARBIE'S DREAM KITCHEN
FIRST TIME PUTTING ON MOM'S CLOTHES
FIRST MASTERY OF JUMP-ROPE
FIRST LOOK AT PLAYBOY
FIRST TIME YOU PUT KEN ON TOP OF BARBIE
FIRST TIME PLAYING DOCTOR
FIRST EXPLANATION OF THE FACTS OF LIFE
FIRST VALENTINE
FIRST SLUMBER PARTY
FIRST CHANGE FROM ANKLETS TO STOCKINGS
FIRST CIGARETTE
FIRST TRAINING BRA
FIRST PUBIC HAIR
FIRST CUP BRA
ARE YOU A MEMBER OF THE B-R-A?
FIRST MAJOR SASSING BACK
FIRST EAR PIERCING
FIRST SHOPLIFTING
FIRST DATE
ARMY
FIRST BASE*
* KISSING
FIRST FRENCH KISS
SECOND BASE*
* OVER AND UNDER BLOUSE
FIRST TIME YOU COME HOME DRUNK OR HIGH
HIYA, FOLKS!!
THIRD BASE*
* DIGITAL-VAGINAL CONTACT
GOING ALL THE WAY
FIRST TIME MOM FINDS BIRTH CONTROL
FIRST JOB
WELCOME TO WEENIE BARN.
MAY I TAKE YOUR ORDER?
FIRST TIME YOU'RE NOT ASKED FOR I.D. IN A BAR
FIRST ABORTION
FIRST MARRIAGE FIRST DIVORCE
FIRST REALIZATION YOU MIGHT NOT WRITE THE GREAT AMERICAN NOVEL BY THE TIME YOU'RE 30
FIRST GRAY HAIR
FIRST TIME CALLED "MA'AM"
ANYTHING ELSE, MA'AM?

About the Author

When unable to think of what to draw, Matt Groening spends his time feeding the ducks that hide in the bushes next to his house. He would like to think that the ducks feel some affection for him, but deep down inside he knows they only love him for his little bits of bread. Despite everything, Groening takes his doodles quite seriously, although he is unsure a cartoonist should really be called an author. These days, Groening resides in Los Angeles—hence the title of his weekly comic strip, *Life in Hell*.

FLASH!

Complete your tour of this hellish life with Matt Groening's other books, all available from HarperCollins.